JOHN THOMPSON'S
EASIEST PIANO COUR

T0081884

FIRST SHOWTUNES

Arranged by Christopher Hussey

ISBN 978-1-5400-3489-2

EXCLUSIVELY DISTRIBUTED BY

HAL•LEONARD®
7777 W. BLUEMOUND RD. P.O. BOX 13819
MILWAUKEE, WISCONSIN 53213

WILLIS MUSIC

Visit Hal Leonard Online at
www.halleonard.com

Contact us:
Hal Leonard
7777 West Bluemound Road
Milwaukee, WI 53213
Email: info@halleonard.com

In Europe, contact:
Hal Leonard Europe Limited
42 Wigmore Street
Marylebone, London, W1U 2RN
Email: info@halleonardeurope.com

In Australia, contact:
Hal Leonard Australia Pty. Ltd.
4 Lentara Court
Cheltenham, Victoria, 3192 Australia
Email: info@halleonard.com.au

Chitty Chitty Bang Bang

from CHITTY CHITTY BANG BANG

Words and Music by Richard M. Sherman
and Robert B. Sherman

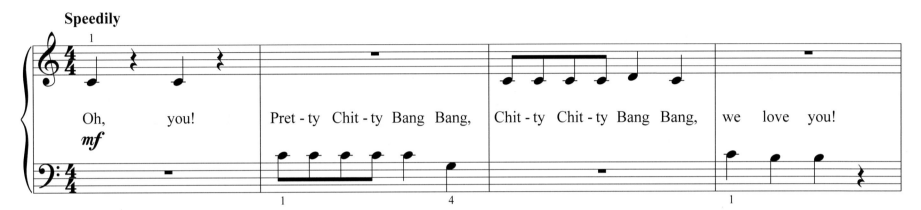

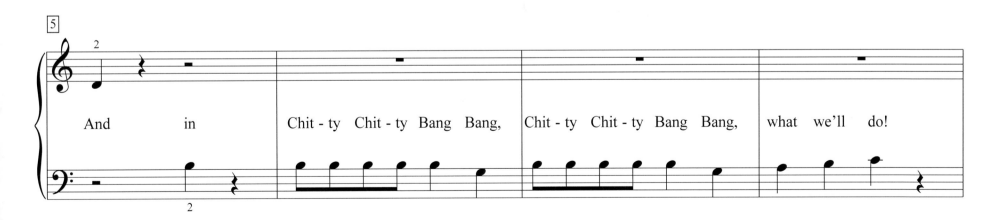

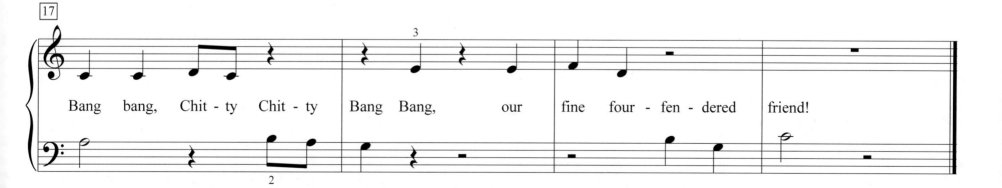

My Favorite Things

from THE SOUND OF MUSIC

Lyrics by Oscar Hammerstein II
Music by Richard Rodgers

When the dog bites, when the bee stings, when I'm feel - ing

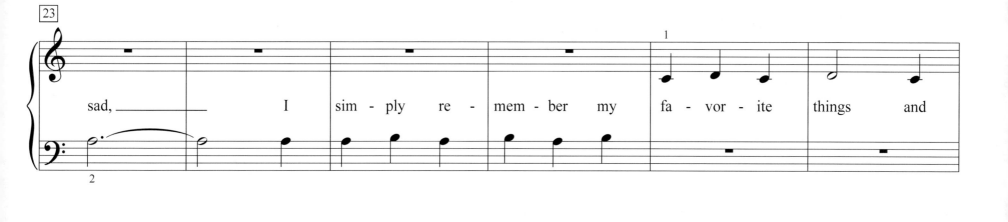

sad, _____ I sim - ply re - mem - ber my fa - vor - ite things and

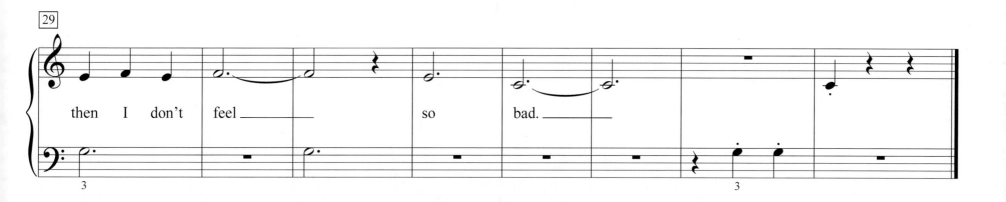

then I don't feel _____ so bad. _____

Over the Rainbow

from THE WIZARD OF OZ

Music by Harold Arlen
Lyric by E.Y. Harburg

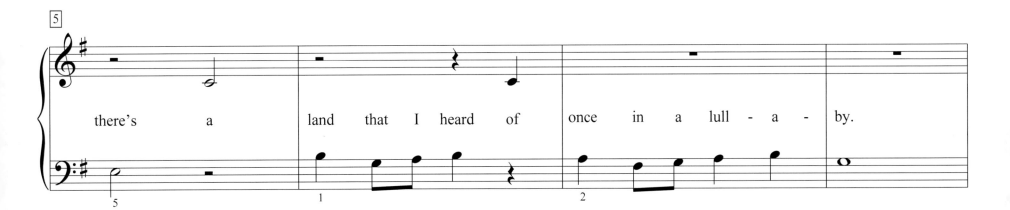

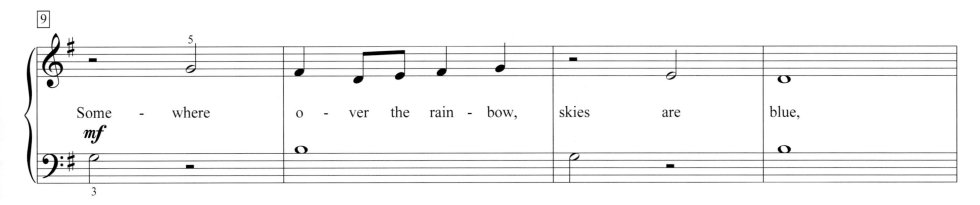

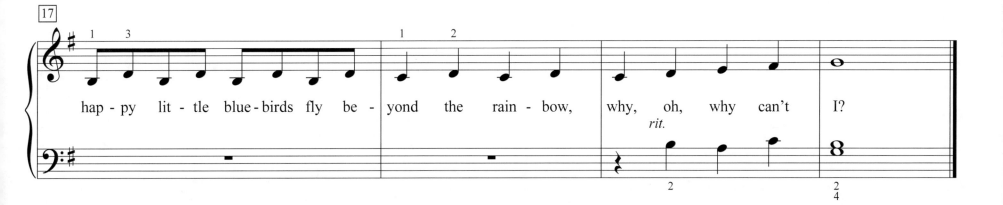

I'd Do Anything
from the Broadway Musical OLIVER!

Words and Music by
Lionel Bart

13

daf - fo - dil?" An - y - thing! "Leave me all your will?" An - y - thing! "E - ven

17

fight my Bill?" What? Fist - i - cuffs? I'd risk ev - 'ry - thing for one kiss,

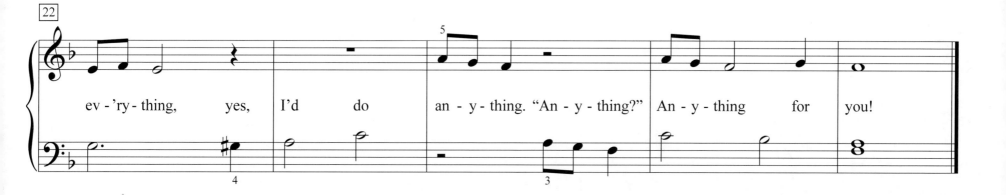

22

ev - 'ry - thing, yes, I'd do an - y - thing. "An - y - thing?" An - y - thing for you!

Be Our Guest
from BEAUTY AND THE BEAST: THE BROADWAY MUSICAL

Music by Alan Menken
Lyrics by Howard Ashman

Cheerfully

Be our guest! Be our guest! Put our ser - vice to the test. Tie your

nap - kin 'round your neck, che - rie, and we pro - vide the rest. *Soup du jour!* Hot *hors*

d'oevres! Why, we on - ly live to serve. Try the grey stuff, it's de - li - cious! Don't be -

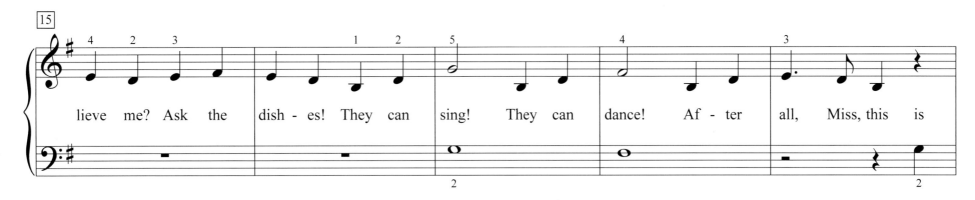

lieve me? Ask the dish - es! They can sing! They can dance! Af - ter all, Miss, this is

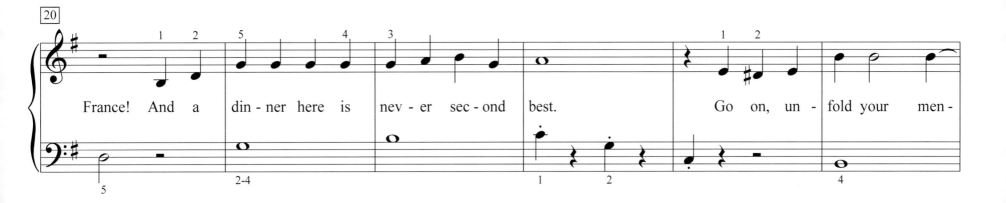

France! And a din - ner here is nev - er sec - ond best. Go on, un - fold your men -

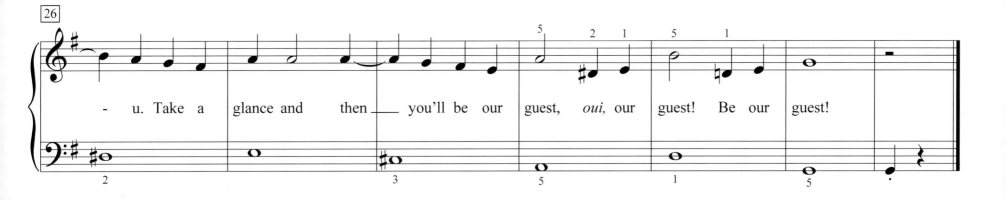

- u. Take a glance and then ___ you'll be our guest, *oui,* our guest! Be our guest!

I Dreamed a Dream
from LES MISÉRABLES

Music by Claude-Michel Schönberg
Lyrics by Alain Boublil, Jean-Marc Natel and Herbert Kretzmer

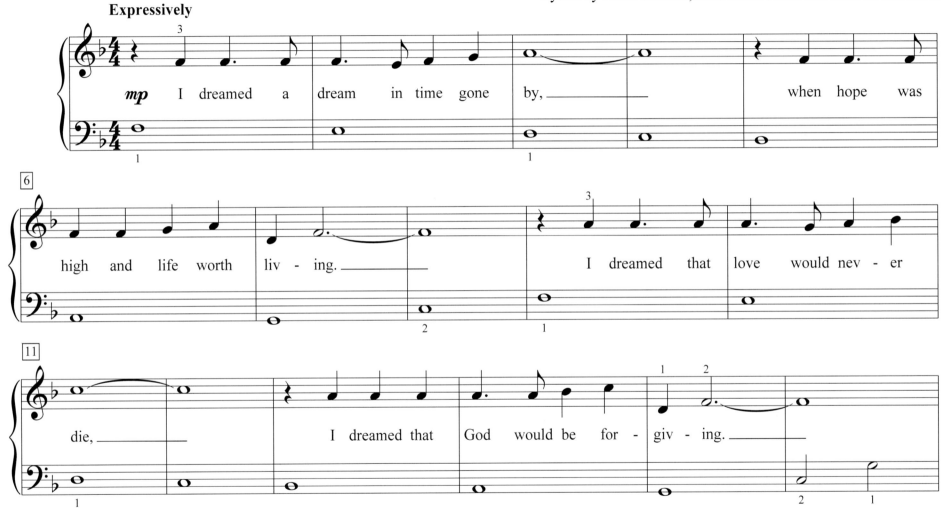

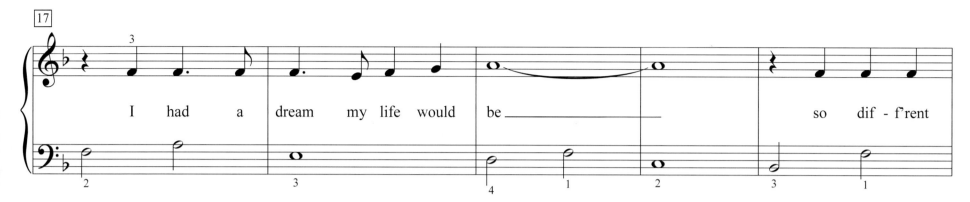

I had a dream my life would be _____ so dif - f'rent

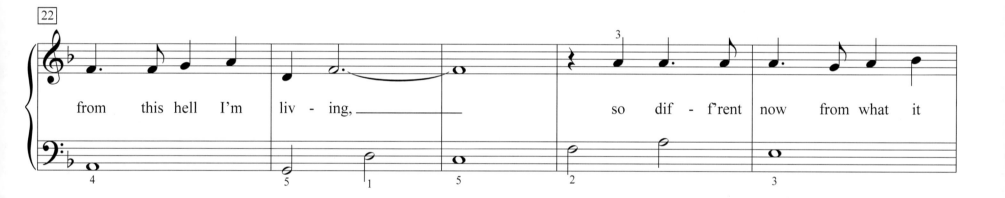

from this hell I'm liv - ing, _____ so dif - f'rent now from what it

seemed. _____ Now life has killed the dream I dreamed. _____

Defying Gravity

from the Broadway Musical WICKED

Music and Lyrics by
Stephen Schwartz

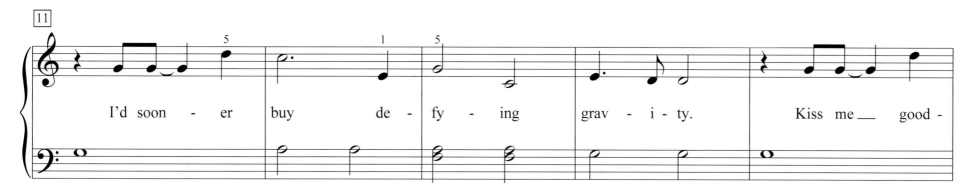

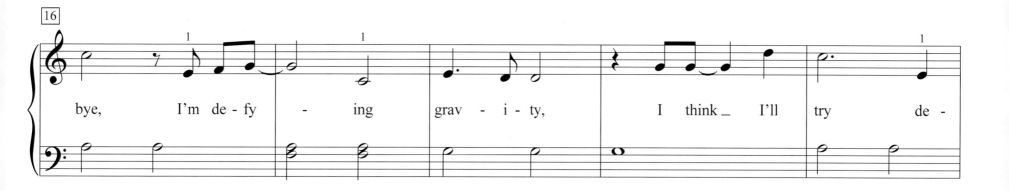

Can You Feel The Love Tonight

from THE LION KING: THE BROADWAY MUSICAL

Music by Elton John
Lyrics by Tim Rice

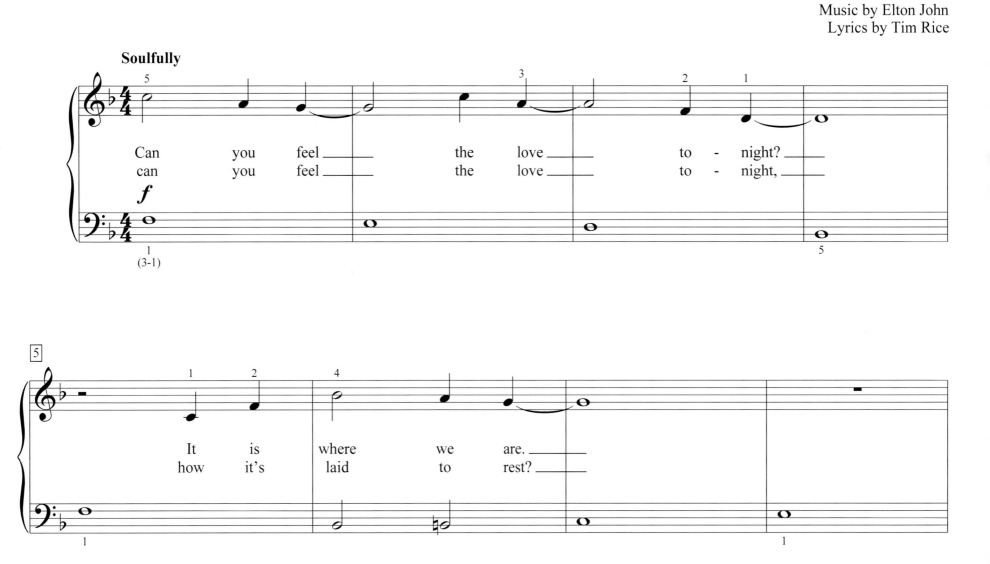

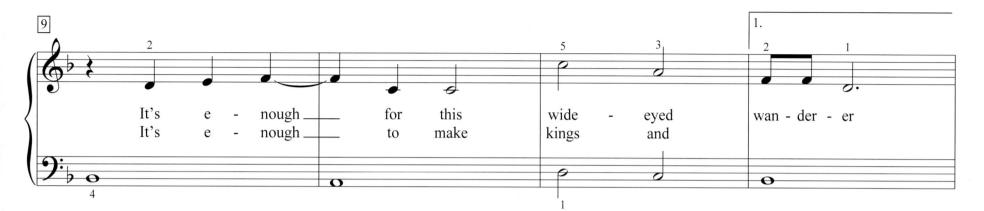

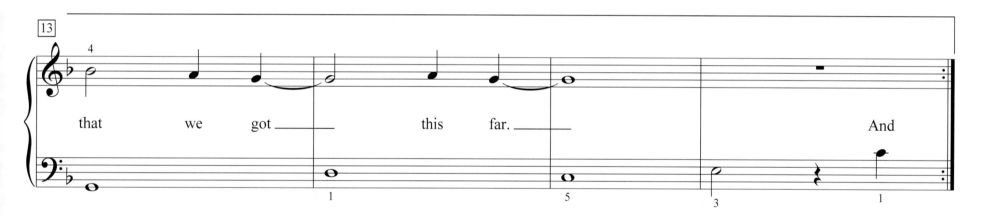

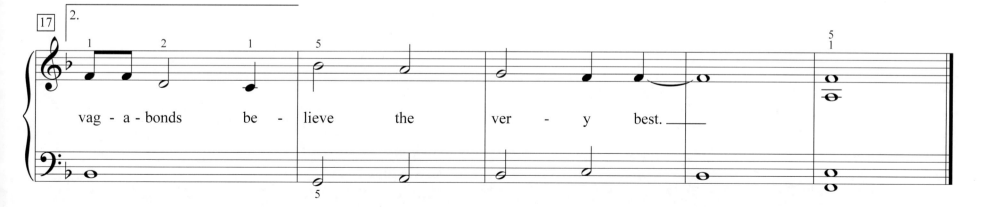

Electricity

from the Broadway Musical BILLY ELLIOT

Music by Elton John
Lyrics by Lee Hall

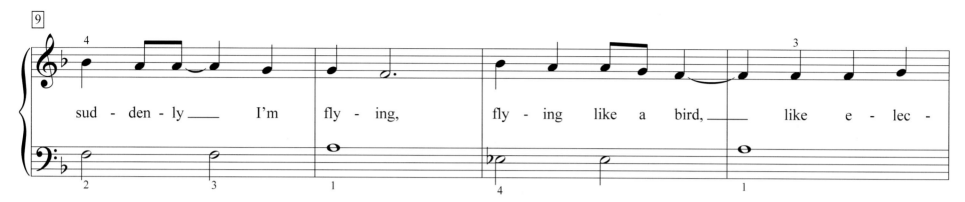

Don't Cry for Me Argentina

from EVITA

Words by Tim Rice
Music by Andrew Lloyd Webber

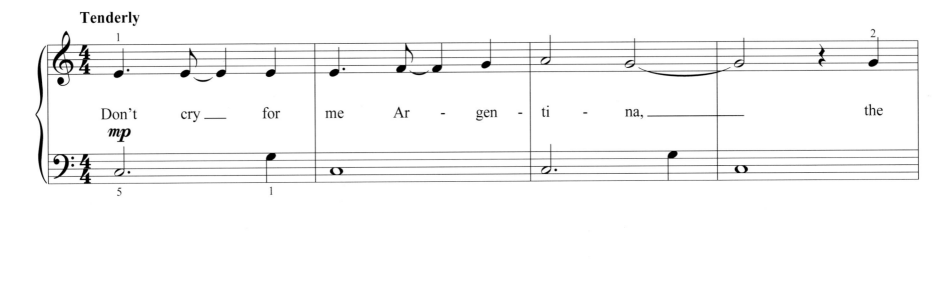

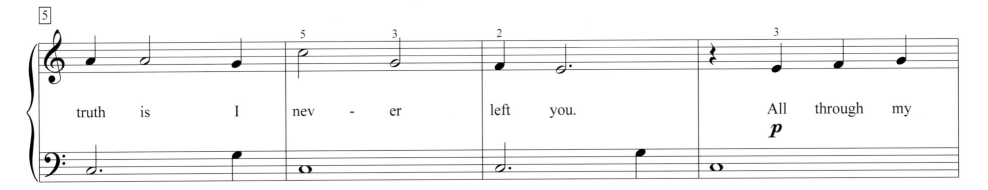

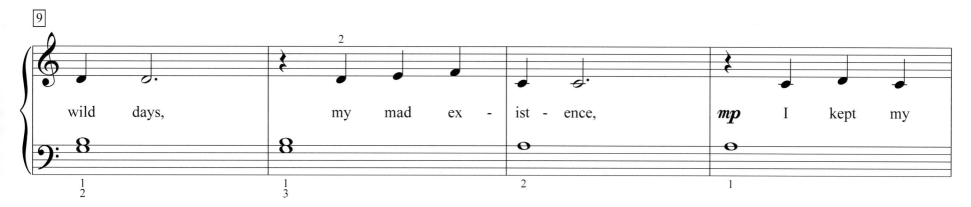

wild days,   my mad ex - ist - ence,   **mp**   I kept my

prom - ise;   don't keep your   dis - tance. _____

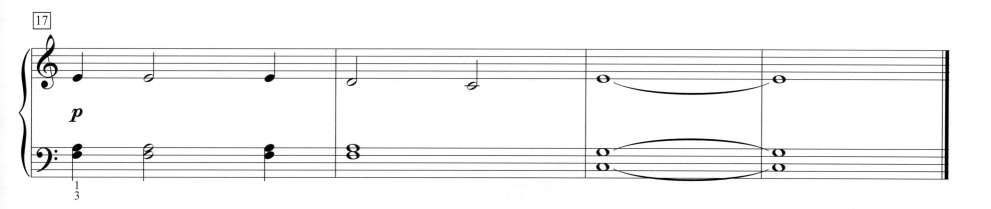

p

Where Is Love?

from the Broadway Musical OLIVER!

Words and Music by
Lionel Bart

Who can say where she may hide? Must I trav-el far and wide

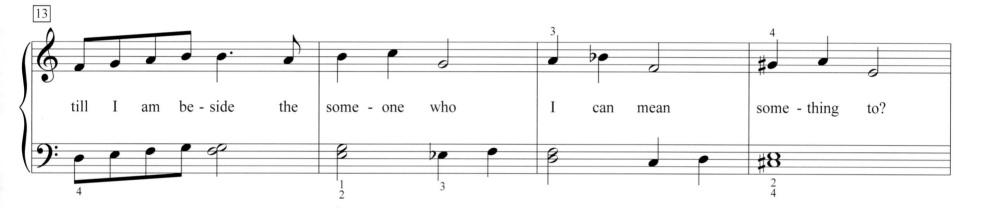

till I am be-side the some-one who I can mean some-thing to?

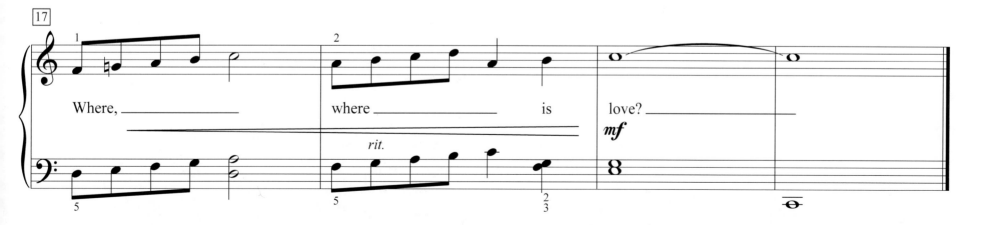

Where, _____ where _____ is love? _____

You'll Never Walk Alone

from CAROUSEL

Lyrics by Oscar Hammerstein II
Music by Richard Rodgers

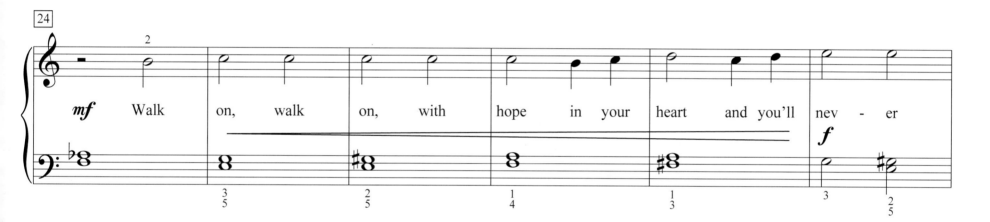

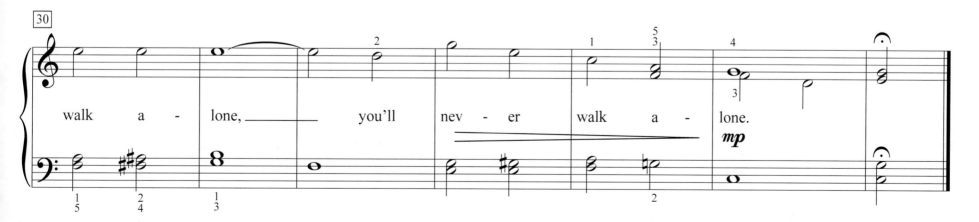

When I Grow Up

from MATILDA THE MUSICAL

Words and Music by
Tim Minchin

on the way to work and I will go to bed late ev - 'ry night.

And I will wake up when the sun comes up, and I will watch car - toons un - til my

eyes go square, and I won't care 'cause I'll be all grown up, when I grow up.

Matchmaker
from the Musical FIDDLER ON THE ROOF

Words by Sheldon Harnick
Music by Jerry Bock

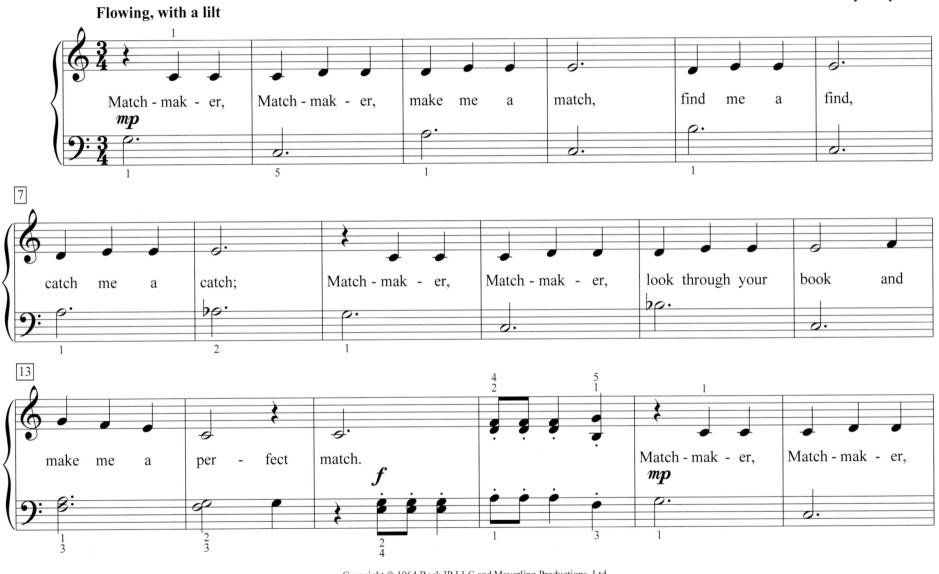

make me a match, find me a find, catch me a catch.

Night af - ter night in the dark I'm a - lone, so find me a match

mf

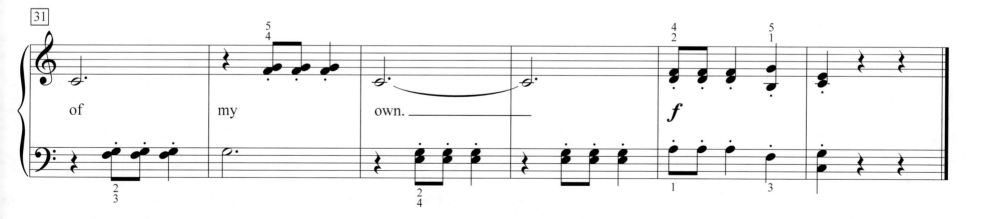

of my own. _____ *f*

A Whole New World

from ALADDIN

Music by Alan Menken
Lyrics by Tim Rice

knew. But when I'm way up here, it's cry - stal clear that now I'm in a

whole new world with you. A whole new world, that's where we'll

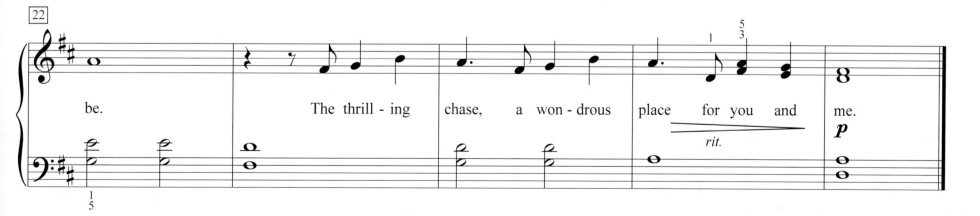

be. The thrill - ing chase, a won - drous place for you and me.

JOHN THOMPSON'S
EASIEST PIANO COURSE

Fun repertoire books are available as an integral part of **John Thompson's Easiest Piano Course**. Graded to work alongside the course, these pieces are ideal for pupils reaching the end of Part 2. They are invaluable for securing basic technique as well as developing musicality and enjoyment.

John Thompson's Easiest Piano Course

00414014	Part 1 – Book only	$6.99
00414018	Part 2 – Book only	$6.99
00414019	Part 3 – Book only	$6.99
00414112	Part 4 – Book only	$6.99

First Pop Songs *arr. Miller*
00416954 .... $8.99

First Classics
00406347 .... $6.99

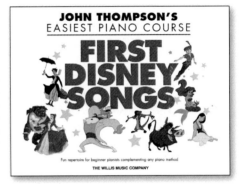

First Disney Songs *arr. Miller*
00416880 .... $9.99

First Jazz Tunes *arr. Baumgartner*
00120872 .... $7.99

First Beethoven *arr. Hussey*
00171709 .... $7.99

First Chart Hits
00141171 .... $7.99

Also available:

First Mozart *arr. Hussey*
00171851 .... $7.99

First Nursery Rhymes
00406229 .... $6.99

First Worship Songs *arr. Austin*
00416892 .... $8.99

Prices, contents and availability subject to change without notice.

Disney characters and artwork © Disney Enterprises Inc.

View complete songlists on **www.halleonard.com**